Desperate Crochet™

Designs by Jennifer McClain

General Information

Many of the products used in this pattern book can be purchased from local craft, fabric and variety stores, or from the Annie's Attic Needlecraft Catalog (see Customer Service information on page 24).

Contents

Sand & Sea Poncho

SKILL LEVEL

INTERMEDIATE

FINISHED SIZE
One size fits most

MATERIALS
- ❑ Caron Simply Soft medium (worsted) weight yarn 96 oz/300 yds/170g per skein): 3 skeins #9703 bone
- ❑ Eyelash bulky (chunky) weight yarn:
    5 oz/175 yds/142g cream
- ❑ Size M/13/9mm wooden crochet hook or size needed to obtain gauge
- ❑ 4 stitch markers or bobby pins

GAUGE
2 sts= 1 inch; 2 sc rows and 1 hdc row = 1½ inches

INSTRUCTIONS

PONCHO

Rnd 1: Holding 1 strand each of bone and cream tog, ch 60, sl st in first ch to form ring, ch 1, sc in each ch around, join with sl st in beg sc, **turn**. Drop cream. *(60 sc)*

Rnd 2: With bone only, ch 1, sc in each st around, join with sl st in beg sc, turn.

Rnd 3 (RS): Ch 2 *(counts as first hdc throughout)*, hdc in each of next 6 sts, 2 hdc in next st, mark 2nd hdc just made, [hdc in each of next 14 sts, 2 hdc in next st, mark 2nd hdc just made] 3 times, hdc in each of last 7 sts, join with sl st in 2nd ch of beg ch-2, turn. *(64 hdc)*

NOTE: *Do not cut unused color; when picking up unused color, always pick up on wrong side of work.*

Rnd 4: Pick up cream; with bone and cream held tog, ch 1, [sc in each st across to next marker, remove marker, 2 sc in st, replace marker in 2nd sc just made] 4 times, sc in each st across, join with sl st in beg sc, turn. Drop cream. *(68 sc)*

Rnd 5: With bone only, ch 1, [sc in each st across to next marker, remove marker, 2 sc in st, replace marker in 2nd sc just made] 4 times, sc in each st across, join with sl st in beg sc, turn. *(72 sc)*

Rnd 6: Ch 2, [hdc in each st across to next marked st, remove marker, 2 hdc in st, replace marker in 2nd hdc just made] 4 times, hdc in each st across, join with sl st in beg sc, turn. *(76 hdc)*

Rnds 7–34: Rep rnds 4–6 consecutively, increasing 4 sts each rnd and ending with 188 sts at end of last rnd. At end of last rnd, fasten off both colors. Remove markers. ❑❑

Glitz & Glamour Scarf

SKILL LEVEL

INTERMEDIATE

FINISHED SIZE
3¼ x 68 inches

MATERIALS
- ❏ Moda Dea Zing metallic fur bulky (chunky) weight yarn (1.75 oz/87 yds/50g per ball): 1 ball #1440 misty
- ❏ Omega 100% nylon size 10 crochet thread: 1 spool white/silver
- ❏ Sizes G/6/4mm and K/10½/ 6.5mm crochet hooks or size needed to obtain gauge
- ❏ Tapestry needle
- ❏ 1 package Bead Treasures Crystal Fancy Mix beads (60g per package)

GAUGE
Size K hook and 1 strand each of yarn and thread held tog: 2 dc and 2 ch-1 sps = 1 inch; 1 dc row = 1 inch

SPECIAL STITCH
V-stitch (V-st): (dc, ch 1, dc) in st indicated.

INSTRUCTIONS

SCARF

Row 1: Holding 1 strand each of misty and white/silver thread tog, with size K hook, ch 15, dc in 5th ch from hook (*first 4 chs count as first dc and ch-1*), [ch 1, sk next ch, dc in next ch] across, turn. (*7 dc, 6 ch-1 sps*)

Row 2: Ch 4 (*counts as first dc and ch 1*), sk next ch sp, [dc in next dc, ch 1, sk next ch sp] 5 times, dc in 3rd ch of ch-4. (*7 dc, 6 ch-1 sps*)

Row 3: Ch 3 (*counts as first dc throughout*), **V-st** (*see Special Stitch*) in each of next 5 dc, dc in 3rd ch of next ch-4, turn. (*5 V-sts, 2 dc*)

Row 4: Ch 4, dc in ch-1 sp of next V-st, [ch 1, dc in ch-1 sp of next V-st] 4 times, ch 1, dc in 3rd ch of ch-4, turn. (*7 dc, 6 ch-1 sps*)

Rows 5–68: Rep rows 2–4 consecutively, ending with row 2. At end of last row, fasten off.

FRINGE

Thread 25 beads onto white/silver thread using a larger-sized bead as first and last beads and alternating sizes as you thread the beads onto the thread. (*If threading is difficult, coat about ¾-inch at end of thread with glue or clear fingernail polish to stiffen the end and make threading easier.*)

Row 69: With size G hook and white/silver, join with sc in first st of row 68, *(ch 20, pull up one bead, ch around bead, ch 20, sc) in same st**, ch 20, pull up one bead, ch around bead, ch 20, sc in next st, rep from * across, ending last rep at **. Fasten off. (*25 fringe*)

Thread 25 more beads onto white/silver thread in same manner as before.

Row 70: Working in starting ch on opposite side of row 1, rep row 69. ❏❏

SKILL LEVEL

INTERMEDIATE

FINISHED SIZE

One size fits most

MATERIALS

- ❑ Paton's Katrina medium (worsted) weight yarn (3.5 oz/163 yds/100g per skein):
    7 skeins #10010 oyster
- ❑ Small amount of white/silver size 10 crochet cotton
- ❑ Size K/101/2/6.5mm crochet hook or size needed to obtain gauge
- ❑ Tapestry needle
- ❑ Beads from Bead Treasures Amethyst Rainbow Mix:
    13 small
    2 medium

GAUGE

2 sts and 1 ch sp = 1 inch sp; 9 rows in pattern = 4 inches

PATTERN NOTE

Always change to new skein of yarn at beginning of a row only, not in the middle.

SPECIAL STITCH

Extended single crochet (esc): Insert hook in st or ch, yo, pull lp through, yo, pull through 1 lp on hook, yo, pull through 2 lps on hook.

INSTRUCTIONS

**VEST
SIDE
MAKE 2.**

Row 1: Ch 111, hdc in 3rd ch from hook, hdc in next ch, [ch 1, sk next ch, **esc** *(see Special Stitch)* in next ch] across to last 3 chs, ch 1, sk next ch, hdc in each of last 2 chs, turn. *(52 esc, 53 ch-1 sps, 4 hdc)*

Rows 2–23: Ch 2 *(counts as first hdc throughout)*, hdc in next hdc, esc in next ch sp, [ch 1, sk next st, esc in next ch sp] across, ending with ch 1, hdc in each of last 2 sts, turn. At end of last row, for **first side**, fasten off; for **2nd side**, turn, **do not fasten off.**

Row 24: For **2nd side only,** ch 2, hdc in next hdc, esc in next ch sp, [ch 1, skip next st, esc in next ch sp] 19 times, turn, **do not fasten off.**

Row 25: For **center back seam,** hold both side pieces tog, matching sts and chs, working through both thicknesses, sl st in each st and in each ch across. Fasten off.

SIDE SEAM

Fold one Side piece in half, matching sts and chs, join with sc in first st at bottom, sc in each of next 25 sts and chs, sl st in next st. Fasten off.
Rep on other Side.

ARMHOLE TRIM

Join with sc in first unworked ch sp at underarm, 3 dc in next ch sp, [sc in next ch sp, 3 dc in next ch sp] around, join with sl st in beg sc.
Rep on other armhole.

EDGING

Rnd 1: Starting at bottom front corner, join with sc in first st, sc in each ch and st across to center back seam, sc in end of row 24, sc in each st and ch on 2nd Side piece to corner, ch 1, working in ends of rows on bottom edge, sc in first row, [ch 2, sk next row or seam, sc in next row] across to other corner, ch 1, join with sl st in beg sc, **do not** turn. Fasten off.

Row 2: Working across bottom edge only, join with sc in first sc after ch-1, 3 dc in next ch-2 sp, [sc in next ch sp, 3 dc in next ch sp] across, sc in last sc before ch-1 at other corner. Fasten off.

TIE CLOSURE

Thread small beads onto size 10 crochet cotton, holding crochet cotton and oyster tog as 1, leaving 6-nch end, [ch 2, pull up bead, ch around bead] 13 times, ch 2. Leaving 6-inch end, fasten off.

Thread 1 medium bead onto 6-inch end of crochet cotton, tie thread and yarn strands tog to secure bead. Using tapestry needle, hide rem 6-inch ends inside closure.

Rep on other end with rem bead.

Insert end of Closure through adjacent ch sps at center front of Vest and loop ends over each other loosely to close.

This Vest can be worn with or without Closure. ❑❑

Glitz & Glamour Brooch

FINISHED SIZE
3 inches in diameter

MATERIALS
- ❏ Omega 100% nylon size 10 thread:
  - 50 yds white/silver
- ❏ 5 yds silver 28-gauge wire
- ❏ Size G/6/4mm crochet hook
- ❏ Sewing needle
- ❏ White sewing thread
- ❏ 6 large assorted beads from Bead Treasures Crystal Fancy Mix
- ❏ Pin back

SPECIAL STITCH
Long stitch (long st): Insert hook through sts of Middle Layer and through Bottom Layer about ½ inch from outer edge of Bottom Layer, complete as sc.

INSTRUCTIONS
BROOCH
BOTTOM LAYER
Rnd 1: With 2 strands nylon thread held tog, ch 2, 7 sc in 2nd ch from hook, join with sl st in beg sc. *(7 sc)*

Rnd 2: Ch 1, 2 sc in first st, 2 hdc in next st, ½ 3 dc in each of next 2 sts, (dc, hdc) in next st, (hdc, sc) in next st, 2 sc in last st, join with sl st in beg sc. *(16 sts)*

Rnd 3: Sl st in next st, (sc, hdc) in next st, (hdc, dc) in next st, 2 dc in each of next 5 sts, (dc, hdc) in next st, 2 hdc in next st, sc in next st, 2 sc in next st, 2 hdc in next st, 2 sc in next st, sl st in each of last 2 sts. Fasten off. *(28 sts)*

MIDDLE LAYER
Saving 1 bead for center, thread rem 5 beads onto 28-gauge wire, ch 5, sl st in first ch to form ring, ch 2, dc in first ch, pull up bead, ch around bead, dc in same ch, dc in next ch, pull up bead, ch around bead, dc in same ch, pull up bead, ch around bead, ch 1, [hdc in next ch, pull up bead, ch around bead] twice, ch 1, sl st in last ch. Fasten off.

TOP LAYER
Rnd 1: With 2 strands thread held tog, ch 2, 7 sc in 2nd ch from hook, join with sl st in beg sc. *(7 sc)*

Rnd 2: Ch 1, sc in first st, ch 1, sc in same st, ch 1, (sc, ch 1) twice in each st around, join with sl st in beg sc. Fasten off.

ASSEMBLY
1. Hold Middle Layer over Bottom Layer matching flat edges, insert wire ends from Middle Layer through sts of Bottom Layer and gently twist tog, being careful not to distort Bottom Layer.

2. With 2 strands nylon thread held tog, join with sl st in last hdc on last rnd of Bottom Layer, sl st in next st, ch 1, **long st** *(see Special Stitch)*, ch 1, sk next st on Bottom Layer, sl st in next st, long st, sk next st on Bottom Layer, sl st in next st, long st, sk next st on Bottom Layer, sl st in next st, [ch 1, sl st in next st] 3 times, *long st, sk next st on Bottom Layer, sl st in next st, [ch 1, sl st in next st] 3 times, rep from *, long st, sk next st on Bottom Layer, [sl st in next st, ch 1] 5 times, sk last st, join with sl st in beg sl st. Fasten off.

3. Position Top Layer over Middle Layer overlapping straight, unbeaded edge of Middle Layer, using thread ends on Top Layer, tack in place leaving edges free.

4. Sew rem bead to center of Top Layer and pin back to center back of Bottom Layer. ❏❏

Peek-a-Boo Poncho

SKILL LEVEL

INTERMEDIATE

FINISHED SIZE

One size fits most

MATERIALS

❑ Paton's Katrina medium (worsted) weight yarn (3.5 oz/163 yds/100g per skein):
  4 skeins #100005 ice
❑ Size M/13/9mm wooden crochet hook or size needed to obtain gauge

GAUGE

3 sts in pattern = 2 inches; 2 pattern rows = 2 inches

PATTERN NOTE

Always change to new skein of yarn at beginning of a row only, not in the middle.

SPECIAL STITCHES

Extended single crochet (esc): Insert hook in st or ch, yo, pull lp through, yo, pull through 1 lp on hook, yo, pull through 2 lps on hook.

Long extended single crochet (long esc): Insert hook in st or ch, yo, pull lp though, [yo, pull through 1 lp on hook] twice, yo, pull through 2 lps on hook.

INSTRUCTIONS

PONCHO

SIDE

MAKE 2.

Row 1: Ch 72, **long esc** *(see Special Stitches)* in 4th ch from hook *(first 3 chs count as first st and ch sp)*, [ch 1, sk next ch, **esc** *(see Special Stitches)* in next ch, ch 1, sk next ch, long esc in next ch] across, turn. *(18 long esc, 18 esc)*

Rows 2–18: Ch 3 *(counts as first st and ch sp)*, [long esc in next st, ch 1, sk next ch sp, esc in next st, ch 1, sk next ch sp] across to last ch-3, long esc in 2nd ch of ch-3, turn. At end of last row, fasten off.

ASSEMBLY

Holding ends of rows on first Side piece to opposite side of row 1 on 2nd Side piece *(see Illustration)*, join with sl st in end of first row on first Side piece, ch 1, sl st in end of first ch sp on 2nd Side piece, ch 1, sl st in end of same row on first Side piece,

[ch 1, sl st in next ch sp on 2nd Side piece, ch 1, sl st in end of next row on first Side piece] across to last ch sp of 2nd Side piece, ch 1, sl st in next ch sp on 2nd Side piece, ch 1, sl st in same row on first Side piece. Fasten off.

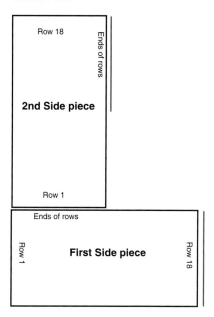

Matching red lines on illustration, rep on opposite ends of Side pieces.

NECK EDGING

Working around neck edge in starting ch and ends of rows, join with sc in any ch sp on opposite side of starting ch on one Side piece, ch 1, [sc in next ch sp, ch 1] around, join with sl st in beg sc. Fasten off.

BOTTOM EDGING

Working around bottom edge in ends of rows, join with sc in any ch sp at seam on one Side piece, ch 1, [sc in next ch sp, ch 1] around, join with sl st in beg sc. Fasten off. ❑❑

Purple Necklace & Earrings

FINISHED SIZES
Necklace: 13 inches long
Earrings: 3¼ inches long

MATERIALS
- ❑ 32-gauge wire:
  5 yds silver
- ❑ Size F/5/3.75mm crochet hook
- ❑ Amethyst Rainbow Mix
  purple glass beads from Bead
  Treasures:
  5 large
  9 medium
  10 small
- ❑ Silver barrel clasp
- ❑ 2 silver fishhook ear wires
- ❑ Scissors

PATTERN NOTES
Do not cut wire until stated in instructions.

Thread 10 beads onto wire in following order: 1 large, 2 medium, 1 small, 1 large, 1 small, 3 medium, 1 large.

INSTRUCTIONS
NECKLACE
PENDANT
Row 1: Leaving 6 inches at beg, with size F hook and wire, place slip knot on hook, pull up first bead, ch around bead positioning knot at top of bead, ch 2, [pull up next medium bead, ch around bead, ch 1] twice, pull up next small bead, ch around bead, ch 3, pull up large bead, ch around bead, ch 3, pull up next small bead, ch around bead, [ch 1, pull up next medium bead, ch around bead] 3 times, ch 2, pull up last large bead, ch around bead, **do not fasten off.**

Row 2: Working back across strand just made, ch 1, sk bead, sl st in each of next 2 chs, [ch 1, sk bead, sl st in next ch] 3 times, ch 1, sk bead, sl st in each of next 3 chs, pulling up lp long enough to match length of large

bead, ch 1, sk bead, sl st in each of next 3 chs, [ch 1, sk next bead, sl st in next ch] twice, ch 1, sk bead, sl st in each of last 2 chs. Leaving 6–inch end, fasten off.

SECURE WIRE
Running wire ends back through large bead, secure ends of wire by running back through large bead several times. Clip end of each strand of wire

as close as possible to bead being careful not to clip stitches.

NECK PIECE
Leaving 6-inch end, with size F hook and wire, place slip knot on hook, ch 35 or until piece measures 7½ inches, sl st around ch at back of large bead in center of Pendant, ch 36 working back across ch just made, sl st in 2nd ch from hook, sl st in each ch across

to bead, sl st in ch at back of bead, sl st in each ch across. Leaving 6-inch end, fasten off.

CONNECTOR PIECE
MAKE 2.

Place Neck Piece with Pendant around neck and measure distance still needed for necklace to hang at desired length (use 6-inch wire ends on back as gauge). Write down measurement still needed, subtract 1 inch from this length and divide rem measurement in half. This is the length you will make each connector piece.

Thread small bead onto wire, leaving 6-inch end, ch number of times needed to equal measurement of connector piece, pull up bead, ch around bead; working back across piece just made, sl st in each ch across to beg. Leaving 6-inch end, fasten off.

ASSEMBLY

1. Using 1 of the 6-inch ends, attach barrel clasp to end of 1 Connector Piece, running wire through lp on clasp several times and back through ch at end of Connector Piece; weave same end of wire through chains of Connector Piece, then insert through bead at end and through end of Neck Piece that does not have long ends rem. (Make sure Neck Piece lays flat and smooth before securing to Connector Piece.)
2. Using same end of wire, secure Neck and Connector Pieces by weaving wire back and forth through chains and bead. Hide ends of wire by inserting them back through bead, then clipping as close as possible to bead.
3. Using the other 6-inch end, attach rem Connector Piece to opposite

end of barrel clasp being careful to keep Neck and Connector Pieces from twisting. Pieces should lay as flat as possible. Weave ends of wire through chain and hide in bead as on first Connector Piece.
4. Using 6-inch ends on Neck Piece, attach beaded end of 2nd Connector Piece to Neck Piece.
5. Cut 6-inch strand of wire and thread through center bead on Pendant Secure center bead in vertical position using 6-inch strand. Hide ends of strand inside bead and clip close to bead.

EARRINGS
RIGHT EARRING

1. Thread beads onto wire in following order: 1 large, 2 small, 1 medium, 1 small, 1 medium.
2. For **Pendant,** leaving 7 inches at beg and end, with wire, place slip knot on hook, pull up first bead, positioning knot at top of bead, ch around bead, ch 1, pull up next bead, ch around bead, ch 3, pull up next bead, ch around bead, ch 2, [pull up next bead, ch around bead, ch 1] twice, pull up last bead, ch around bead allowing ch to slide back to top of bead, ch 1, working back across piece just made, sl st in next ch, [ch 1, sk next bead, sl st in next ch] twice, sl st in next ch, ch 1, sk next bead, sl st in each of next 3 chs, ch 1, sk next bead, sl st in last ch. Fasten off.
3. Weave 1 of the 7-inch ends on earring piece through chs to medium bead at center. Gently fold Pendant at medium bead, using same 7–inch end, attach 1 ear wire to medium bead by running wire back and forth through bead and around lp on bottom of ear wire, wrapping wire

around strands between lp and bead as needed to secure. Hide end inside bead and clip close to bead.
4. Weave rem 7-inch end through bead and ch at end until secure, hide end inside bead and clip. (If ch lp on end bead becomes too loose, use 7-inch end to pull lp up, then secure.)

LEFT EARRING

1. Thread beads onto wire in following order: 1 medium, 1 small, 1 medium, 2 small, 1 large.
2. For **Pendant,** leaving 7-inches at beg and end, with wire, place slip knot on hook, pull up first bead, positioning knot at top of bead, ch around bead, [ch 1, pull up next bead, ch around bead] twice, ch 2, pull up next bead, ch around bead, ch 3, pull up next bead, ch around bead, ch 1, pull up last bead, ch around bead allowing ch to slide back to top of bead, ch 1, working back across piece just made, sl st in next ch, ch 1, sk next bead, sl st in each of next 3 chs, ch 1, sk next bead, sl st in each of next 2 chs, [ch 1, sk next bead, sl st in next ch] twice. Fasten off.
3. Weave 1 of the 7-inch ends on earring piece through chs to medium bead at center. Gently fold Pendant at medium bead, using same 7-inch end, attach 1 ear wire to medium bead by running wire back and forth through bead and around lp on bottom of ear wire, wrapping wire around strands between lp and bead as needed to secure. Hide end inside bead and clip close to bead.
4. Weave rem 7-inch end through bead and ch at end until secure, hide end inside bead and clip. (If ch lp on end bead becomes too loose, use 7-inch end to pull lp up, then secure.) ❑❑

Shimmery Shoulder Shrug

FINISHED SIZE
10 x 57 inches

MATERIALS
- ❑ Aunt Lydia's Shimmer Fashion fine (sport) weight yarn (2 oz/124 yds/57g per ball): 4 balls light linen
- ❑ Lion Brand Fun Fur Prints bulky (chunky) weight yarn (1.50 oz/57 yds/40g per ball): 2 balls #205 sandstone
- ❑ Sizes H/8/5mm and M/13/9mm crochet hooks or size needed to obtain gauge
- ❑ Sewing needle
- ❑ White sewing thread
- ❑ 5 yds silver 28 gauge wire
- ❑ Coordinating color beads: 7 medium size 3 larger novelty type
- ❑ 9 inches of ¼-inch-wide white elastic

GAUGE
Size M hook: 2 sts = 1 inch; 4 sc rows = 2 inches.

INSTRUCTIONS
SHRUG
Row 1: Holding 2 strands of light linen and 1 strand of sandstone tog as 1, with size M hook, ch 90, drop sandstone; with 2 strands light linen only, sc in 2nd ch from hook, [sk next ch, 2 sc in next ch] across, turn. Leaving 7-inch end for fringe, fasten off sandstone. *(89 sc)*

Rows 2 & 3: Ch 1, sc in first st, [sk next st, 2 sc in next st] across, turn.

Row 4: Holding 1 strand sandstone and 2 strands light linen tog, ch 1, sc in first st, [sk next st, 2 sc in next st] across, turn. Leaving 7-inch end for fringe, fasten off sandstone.

Rows 5–7: Ch 1, sc in first st, [sk next st, 2 sc in next st] across, turn.

Rows 8–20: Rep rows 4–7 consecutively, ending with row 4. At end of last row, fasten off.

EDGING
With 2 strands light linen and 1 strand sandstone held tog and RS of row 20 facing, working in ends of rows across 1 end of Shrug, join with sc in first row, sc in each row across. Fasten off.

Rep on opposite end.

FRINGE
Cut 40 strands each of light linen and sandstone 15 inches in length. Holding 1 strand of each color tog, fold in half, pull fold through, pull ends through fold, pulling long ends into fringe where needed. Trim ends even. Fringe across each short end.

CLOSURE RING
With white thread and sewing needle, overlapping ends ½-inch, sew ends of elastic tog to form ring.

With 2 strands light linen and 1 strand sandstone held tog and size M hook, leaving 7-inch end, join with sc around elastic ring *(see illustrations)*, 39 more sc around ring, join with sl st in beg sc. Leaving 7-inch end, fasten off. Tie 7-inch ends in square knot and leave ends long.

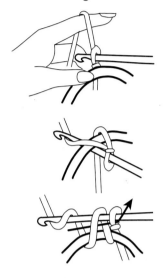

Sc around ring

FREEFORM ORNAMENT
BASE
Rnd 1: With 2 strands light linen held tog and size H hook, leaving 7-inch ends, ch 4, 9 dc in 4th ch from hook *(first 3 chs count as first dc)*, join with sl st in 3rd ch of beg ch-4. *(10 dc)*

Rnd 2: [Ch 3, sl st in next st] 7 times, for **top**, ch 1, 2 sc in next st, 2 hdc in next st, ch 1, join with sl st in first st of rnd 1. Leaving 7-inch ends, fasten off. Pull ends to back of work.

TOP
Rnd 1: Thread 7 medium beads onto 28-gauge wire. Leave 7-inch ends at beg and end of wire, with size H hook, ch 3, 3 sc in 2nd ch from hook, 2 sc in last ch; working on opposite side of ch, 3 sc in same ch, 2 sc in last ch, join with sl st in beg sc. *(10 sc)*

Rnd 2: Ch 1, sc in first st, pull up bead, ch around bead, ch 1, sl st in next sc, ch 1, sc in same st, [pull up bead, ch around bead, ch 1, sc in next st] twice, pull up bead, ch around bead, ch 1, sl st in next sc,

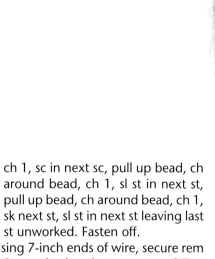

ch 1, sc in next sc, pull up bead, ch around bead, ch 1, sl st in next st, pull up bead, ch around bead, ch 1, sk next st, sl st in next st leaving last st unworked. Fasten off.

Using 7-inch ends of wire, secure rem 3 novelty beads to center of Top piece *(see close-up photo)*; **do not** clip ends of wire.

Position Top over Base with joining of rnd 2 on Top over hdc sts of rnd 2 on Base, push rem ends of wire on top through sts of Base. Being careful not to distort sts of either piece, twist ends of wire tog for length of ends forming one piece of wire. Curl this twisted piece of wire around end of hook forming a ring, then gently press ring into center of Ornament.

Using 7-inch ends on Base piece and square knot, tie Base to Closure Ring at joining, tie ends a 2nd time so knot is positioned at bottom of Base.

Slip ends of Shrug through Closure Ring and position on shoulders as desired. ❑❑

Wrapped Up In You

FINISHED SIZE
45 x 55 inches

MATERIALS
- ❑ Red Heart Symphony medium (worsted) weight yarn (3.5 oz/310 yds/100g per skein):
  - 3 skeins #4903 mystic purple
- ❑ Size M wooden crochet hook or size needed to obtain gauge

GAUGE
13 sts = 6 inches, 6 rows in pattern = 5 inches

INSTRUCTIONS

AFGHAN

Row 1: Ch 92, sc in 2nd ch from hook, ch 1, sk next ch, dc in next ch, [ch 1, sk next ch, sc in next ch, ch 1, sk next ch, dc in next ch] across, turn. *(23 sc, 23 dc, 45 chs)*

Row 2: Ch 1, sc in first dc, ch 1, sk next ch, dc in next sc, [ch 1, sk next ch, sc in next dc, ch 1, sk next ch, dc in next sc] across, turn.

Row 3: Ch 1, sc in first dc, [3 dc in next sc, sc in next dc] across to last sc, 2 dc in last sc, turn. *(23 sc, 23 3-dc groups)*

Row 4: Ch 1, sc in first dc, ch 1, sk next st, dc in next sc, [ch 1, sk next st, sc in next dc, ch 1, sk next st, dc in next sc] across, turn.

Rows 5–68: Rep rows 2–4 consecutively, ending with row 2. At end of last row, **do not turn or fasten off.**

Rnd 69: Working in sts and in ends of rows around outer edge, ch 3 *(counts as first dc)*, 6 dc in top of last st, *[sk end of next row, sc in next row, sk next row, 5 dc in next row] across to last 4 rows, sk end of next row, sc in next row, sk next row, 7 dc in last row *; working on opposite side of row 1, sc in next dc, [5 dc in next sc, sc in next dc] across to last sc, sk last sc, 7 dc in last dc, rep between *, [sc in next dc, 5 dc in next sc] across to last 2 sts, **sc dec** *(see Stitch Guide)* in last 2 sts, join with sl st in 3rd ch of beg ch-3. Fasten off. ❑❑

Midnight Pansies Stole & Bag

SKILL LEVEL

INTERMEDIATE

FINISHED SIZE
Stole: 5½ x 56 inches

MATERIALS
- ❑ Lion Brand Moonlight Mohair bulky (chunky) weight yarn (1.75 oz/82 yds/50g per skein): 2 skeins #206 purple mountains
- ❑ Sizes F/5/3.75mm and M/13/ 9mm crochet hooks or size needed to obtain gauge
- ❑ Tapestry needle
- ❑ Sewing needle
- ❑ Purple sewing thread
- ❑ Small amount silver 32-gauge wire
- ❑ Purple beads:
    10 small
    2 medium
- ❑ Purple elastic ponytail holder *(about 1 inch across)*
- ❑ Pin back
- ❑ Small black handbag

GAUGE
Size M hook and mohair: 2 sts = 1 inch; 1 dc row = 1 inch

INSTRUCTIONS

STOLE
Row 1: For foundation chain, with size M hook, ch 4, dc in 4th ch from hook, **turn,** *ch 3, dc in dc, **turn,** rep from * 21 times. *(23 ch sps)*

Row 2: Working in ch sps along foundation chain, ch 4 *(counts as first dc and ch-1)*, (dc, ch 1, dc, ch 1) in each ch sp across, dc in first ch of first ch-4 on foundation, turn. *(48 dc, 47 ch sps)*

Rows 3–5: Ch 4, dc in next ch sp, [ch 1, dc in next ch sp] across, turn.

Rnd 6: Working around entire outer edge, ch 1, (sc, ch 2, sc) in each ch sp across to last ch sp, (sc, ch 2, sc, ch 2, sc) in last ch sp; *working in ends of rows, (sc, ch 2, sc) in each of next 3 rows*; working in ch sps on foundation chain, (sc, ch 2, sc) in each ch sp across, rep between *, sc in end of last row, ch 2, join with sl st in beg sc. Fasten off.

PANSY
MAKE 2
Rnd 1: With size M hook, ch 3, sl st in first ch to form ring, ch 1, [sc in ring, ch 3] 5 times, join with sl st in beg sc. *(5 ch-3 sps)*

Rnd 2: Working behind ch-3 sps of rnd 1 into center ring, *(hdc, 3 dc, hdc) between next 2 sc, sc around **post** *(see Stitch Guide)* of next sc, rep from *, **(hdc, dc, 3 tr, dc, hdc) between next 2 sc, sc around post of next sc, rep from ** twice. Leaving 12-inch end, fasten off.

Thread 12-inch end into tapestry needle; weave through sts of rnd 2 and pull, closing up center hole on rnd 1, **do not cut ends.**

CENTER
Thread 1 medium bead onto 32-gauge wire, then 5 small beads, with size F hook, ch 5, sl st in first ch to form ring, [sc in ring, pull up small bead, ch around bead, ch 3] twice, [sc in ring, ch 2, pull up small bead, ch around bead, ch 2] 3 times, sc in ring, ch 1, pull up medium bead, ch around bead, ch 1. Fasten off.

Fold last bead over center of ring and twist ends of wire tog lightly on back of Center. Insert wire ends through center of Pansy, coil into a small *(dime-sized)* ring and stitch in place using rem of 12-inch end on Pansy; using same end, loosely tack several loops of Center to Pansy to secure, **do not cut end of yarn.**

STOLE CLOSURE
Position ponytail holder over back of Pansy, covering ring of wire from Center; sew in place securely. Hide and clip ends of yarn.

BAG ORNAMENT
Sew pin back to wrong side of Pansy, covering ring of wire. Hide and clip ends of yarn.

Pin to handbag. ❑❑

Crochet Stitch Guide

ABBREVIATIONS

beg	begin/beginning
bpdc	back post double crochet
bpsc	back post single crochet
bptr	back post treble crochet
CC	contrasting color
ch	chain stitch
ch-	refers to chain or space previously made (i.e. ch-1 space)
ch sp	chain space
cl	cluster
cm	centimeter(s)
dc	double crochet
dec	decrease/decreases/decreasing
dtr	double treble crochet
fpdc	front post double crochet
fpsc	front post single crochet
fptr	front post treble crochet
g	gram(s)
hdc	half double crochet
inc	increase/increases/increasing
lp(s)	loop(s)
MC	main color
mm	millimeter(s)
oz	ounce(s)
pc	popcorn
rem	remain/remaining
rep	repeat(s)
rnd(s)	round(s)
RS	right side
sc	single crochet
sk	skip(ped)
sl st	slip stitch
sp(s)	space(s)
st(s)	stitch(es)
tog	together
tr	treble crochet
trtr	triple treble
WS	wrong side
yd(s)	yard(s)
yo	yarn over

Chain—ch: Yo, pull through lp on hook.

Slip stitch—sl st: Insert hook in st, yo, pull through both lps on hook.

Single crochet—sc: Insert hook in st, yo, pull through st, yo, pull through both lps on hook.

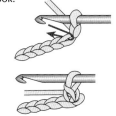

**Front loop—front lp
Back loop—back lp**

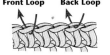

Front post stitch—fp: Back post stitch—bp: When working post st, insert hook from right to left around post st on previous row.

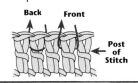

Half double crochet—hdc: Yo, insert hook in st, yo, pull through st, yo, pull through all 3 lps on hook.

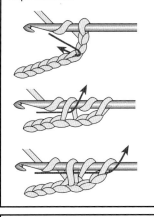

Double crochet—dc: Yo, insert hook in st, yo, pull through st, [yo, pull through 2 lps] twice.

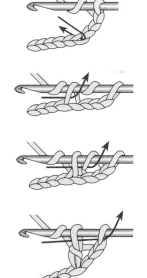

Change colors: Drop first color; with second color, pull through last 2 lps of st.

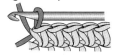

Treble crochet—tr: Yo twice, insert hook in st, yo, pull through st, [yo, pull through 2 lps] 3 times.

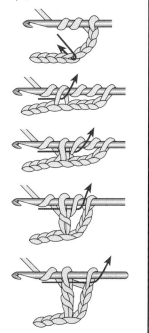

Double treble crochet—dtr: Yo 3 times, insert hook in st, yo, pull through st, [yo, pull through 2 lps] 4 times.

Single crochet decrease (sc dec): (Insert hook, yo, draw up a lp) in each of the sts indicated, yo, draw through all lps on hook.

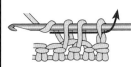

Example of 2-sc dec

Half double crochet decrease (hdc dec): (Yo, insert hook, yo, draw lp through) in each of the sts indicated, yo, draw through all lps on hook.

Example of 2-hdc dec

Double crochet decrease (dc dec): (Yo, insert hook, yo, draw lp through, yo, draw through 2 lps on hook) in each of the sts indicated, yo, draw through all lps on hook.

Example of 2-dc dec

US		UK
sl st (slip stitch)	=	sc (single crochet)
sc (single crochet)	=	dc (double crochet)
hdc (half double crochet)	=	htr (half treble crochet)
dc (double crochet)	=	tr (treble crochet)
tr (treble crochet)	=	dtr (double treble crochet)
dtr (double treble crochet)	=	ttr (triple treble crochet)
skip	=	miss

For more complete information, visit

StitchGuide.com

Fringe

Cut a piece of cardboard half as long as specified in instructions for strands plus ½ inch for trimming. Wind yarn loosely and evenly around cardboard. When cardboard is filled, cut yarn across one end. Do this several times then begin fringing. Wind additional strands as necessary.

SINGLE KNOT FRINGE

Hold specified number of strands for one knot together, fold in half. Hold project to be fringed with right side facing you. Use crochet hook to draw folded end through space or stitch indicated from right to wrong side.

Pull loose ends through folded section. Draw knot up firmly. Space knots as indicated in pattern instructions.

Single Knot Fringe

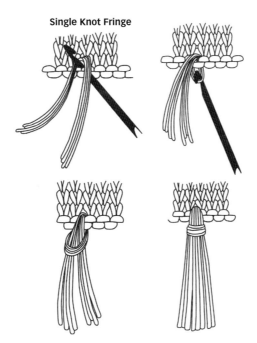

DOUBLE KNOT FRINGE

Begin by working Single Knot Fringe completely across one end of piece. With right side facing you and working from left to right, take half the strands of one knot and half the strands of the knot next to it and knot them together.

Double Knot Fringe

TRIPLE KNOT FRINGE

Work Double Knot Fringe across. On the right side, work from left to right tying a third row of knots.

Triple Knot Fringe

Standard Yarn Weight System

Categories of yarn, gauge ranges, and recommended needle sizes

Yarn Weight Symbol & Category Names	1 SUPER FINE	2 FINE	3 LIGHT	4 MEDIUM	5 BULKY	6 SUPER BULKY
Type of Yarns in Category	Sock, Fingering, Baby	Sport, Baby	DK, Light Worsted	Worsted, Afghan, Aran	Chunky, Craft, Rug	Bulky, Roving
Knit Gauge* Ranges in Stockinette Stitch to 4 inches	21–32 sts	23–26 sts	21–24 sts	16–20 sts	12–15 sts	6–11 sts
Recommended Needle in Metric Size Range	2.25–3.25mm	3.25–3.75mm	3.75–4.5mm	4.5–5.5mm	5.5–8mm	8mm
Recommended Needle U.S. Size Range	1 to 3	3 to 5	5 to 7	7 to 9	9 to 11	11 and larger

* GUIDELINES ONLY: The above reflect the most commonly used gauges and hook sizes for specific yarn categories.

Skill Levels

◼◻◻◻◻ **BEGINNER**
Beginner projects using basic stitches. Minimal shaping.

◼◼◻◻◻ **EASY**
Projects using basic stitches, repetitive stitch patterns, simple color changes and simple shaping and finishing.

◼◼◼◻◻ **INTERMEDIATE**
Projects with a variety of stitches, mid-level shaping and finishing.

◼◼◼◼◻ **EXPERIENCED**
Projects using advanced techniques and stitches, more intricate lace patterns and numerous color changes.

306 East Parr Road
Berne, IN 46711
© 2005 Annie's Attic

TOLL-FREE ORDER LINE or to request a free catalog (800) LV-ANNIE (800) 582-6643
Customer Service (800) AT-ANNIE (800) 282-6643, **Fax** (800) 882-6643
Visit www.AnniesAttic.com

ISBN: 1-59635-047-4   Printed in USA   1 2 3 4 5 6 7 8 9